ONCE UPON A FULL MOON

ONCE UPON A FULL MOON

ELIZABETH QUAN

Tundra Books

Published in Canada by Tundra Books,
75 Sherbourne Street, Toronto, Ontario M5A 2P9

Published in the United States by Tundra Books of Northern New York,
P.O. Box 1030, Plattsburgh, New York 12901

Library of Congress Control Number: 2006906056

Library and Archives Canada Cataloguing in Publication

Quan, Elizabeth, 1921-
    Once upon a full moon / Elizabeth Quan.

ISBN 978-0-88776-813-2

        1. Quan, Elizabeth, 1921-   Travel – China – Juvenile literature.
2. China – Description and travel – Juvenile literature.   I. Title.

DS710.Q82 2007   j915.104'41   C2006-903783-3

We acknowledge the financial support of the Government of Canada through the
Book Publishing Industry Development Program (BPIDP) and that of the Government of
Ontario through the Ontario Media Development Corporation's Ontario Book Initiative.

We further acknowledge the support of the Canada Council for
the Arts and the Ontario Arts Council for our publishing program.

ONTARIO ARTS COUNCIL
CONSEIL DES ARTS DE L'ONTARIO

Medium: watercolor on paper

Design: Terri Nimmo

Printed and bound in China

1 2 3 4 5 6   12 11 10 09 08 07

To the Lee King family and their descendants

THIS IS THE TRUE STORY of a Chinese family in the 1920s who made the trip across Canada and the Pacific Ocean to inland China. It is the story of a journey in a time before jet and diesel. It is the story of a devoted father, whose courage and joy took us all safely across the miles to our destination – Grandmother's house – losing only one child's hat.

Through the window by my bed, the man in the moon beamed a big smile. His light shone as I tossed and turned, thinking of the exciting news. *China! Grandmother!* My little world was beginning to spin.

Papa came and sat on my bed. "When next you see the full moon, it will be at Grandmother's house far away," he said. I knew about grandmothers from the story of Little Red Riding Hood, but I didn't know my own.

In the morning I stood on a stool and, reaching up and up, drew a picture of a person taller than Papa. I made long arms, ready for a huge embrace, and put a big smile on her face, showing how happy she was to see us.

Papa bought new dresses for the girls, new shoes for the boys, and a new cream-colored hat for Mama, wound about with a veil and sprinkled with pearly beads. We tried it on; Mama would be beautiful in it.

Papa was our barber. With scissors and clippers, he gave the boys a cut that never needed comb or brush. For the girls, a blunt bob with bangs. Our hair made us look foreign among our friends.

Then Mama began to pack. She pulled out the big black trunk that had been George's bed, and another, smaller blue one. Into these went clothing, and gifts for Grandmother. Mama then stuffed two duffel bags with bedding and pillows. Two leather suitcases, one yellow and one red, held a change of clothes for each of us. George squeezed in his Meccano set and I slipped in my crayons. If Mama knew, she didn't say anything.

Papa tied the duffel bags with rope and buckled the trunks and suitcases. We watched as he took a bottle of black ink, dipped his big brush, and lettered *L.K.* on each piece. "That stands for Lee King," he told us, "the name they gave me when I first came to Canada. It should have been King Lee. In China the family name comes first, but here the backwards name stuck."

We climbed that mountain of luggage. Peter sat on top of the duffel bag, riding it like a pony. I grew to love the sight of that pile. It made me feel as if I belonged to something, even when we were on the move and had no place to call home. *L.K.* meant that it was ours. We were part of it.

The full moon lit the sky as we boarded the train in Toronto. Our coach had nothing but bunks with curtains, so we all went to bed. My sister Gerry and I climbed to a top berth. The jerks and bumps and funny smells made us feel sick. I missed my own bed. *Would it be like this all the way to Grandmother's house?*

Morning came. With a flip of his wrist, the porter changed our beds to seats and brought a table. Papa produced lumpy parcels. What treats! We kicked our heels happily as we bit into white bread and butter – spread with thick strawberry jelly – cookies, and tangerines.

Next day, the conductor walked through the coach calling, "Winnipeg, coming up! You will have time to go into the city."

Papa had crossed the country before. He knew just where to go. At the restaurant he ordered old fire winter-melon soup with tofu, fish balls with black-bean sauce, lightly cooked greens, and white rice – the kind of simple food we ate every day at home.

When it came, steamy hot, Papa picked up his bowl and chopsticks and ate hungrily. Mama served us, but hardly touched the food herself.

At first, I pouted. "I'd rather have bread and jelly," I said, but then I took up the long awkward chopsticks, picked up a fish ball, and popped it into my mouth. I was proud of myself. At home I'd had the short little sawed-off chopsticks of a child.

There were other stops across the prairies. We would step out onto the small platform and stamp up and down in the cold air. In the mountains, sometimes we could see the engine and sometimes we could see the caboose, along the twisting track.

When we approached the forested foothills, we looked for animals and saw a mountain goat and a moose. Grandmother's house seemed very far away.

We had been traveling for four days and five nights. Then we reached the sea. While we waited for the ship that would carry us across the Pacific Ocean, Papa took Gerry and me to the Cantonese Opera. The acrobats, the colors, the music of the wailing Chinese strings punctuated with drums and cymbals, the stories of kings and emperors, of loves and wars and victories, took him back to the China of long, long ago.

"As a boy I used to watch, standing among the farmers fresh from the fields, still carrying their hoes," he told us.

The moon was a sliver when we boarded the ship. We traveled in its bowels, in the section set aside for Orientals. We were the only family. They put up a canvas curtain, enclosing our bunks and making a cozy little corner room. It divided us from all the other passengers, mostly single men. Gerry and I stood on our upper bunk and peeked over the curtain at the others, all lying in bunk beds row upon row. Papa scolded us.

"Whales!"

Everyone clanged up the metal stairs to stare at the dark forms diving and blowing in the distance. Sometimes at dusk I would go up alone and stand at the railing, but I never saw the whales again.

Steadily we plowed westward, closer to Grandmother every day. Finally, to the call of seabirds, out of the mist appeared a blue-green land. We had reached Japan.

"This is the other side of the world," said Mama. "Yokohama. I have an old friend who lives near the docks. We will go to visit her while the ship is unloading and then reboard." She put on her new hat, and we wobbled down the gangway on our sea legs, right into a storybook world.

Gaily dressed ladies minced along on wooden clogs, speaking a language we did not understand. Someone directed us into a side street. A charming thatched-roof house sat among shrubbery, a willow tree in front.

Mama greeted her friend warmly. We took off our shoes and stepped onto the tatami. A little girl led Gerry outside to play while the rest of us settled ourselves on pretty cushions.

"Ah!" Mama's friend sighed, pouring green tea into teeny cups and passing bite-sized cakes. "My daughter is becoming more and more Japanese. She doesn't want to speak Chinese anymore."

I heard the peals of laughter outdoors. The short afternoon soon drew to a close. *"Sayonara! Joy gin!"* the family called out, clustering at the door. "Good-bye and come again!"

"Soon we will be at Grandmother's house," said Papa, as he lounged in his bunk.

The sun shone brighter every day as we headed toward Kwangtung, the southernmost province of China.

"Tell us about when you were a little boy!" we urged him.

So, through leisurely days, Papa talked about how he had to leave school early and work as a cowherd, about how his father in California often did not send money home. "When I turned seventeen, a distant uncle sent me a ticket to join him in Canada. I cut off my pigtail as soon as I arrived."

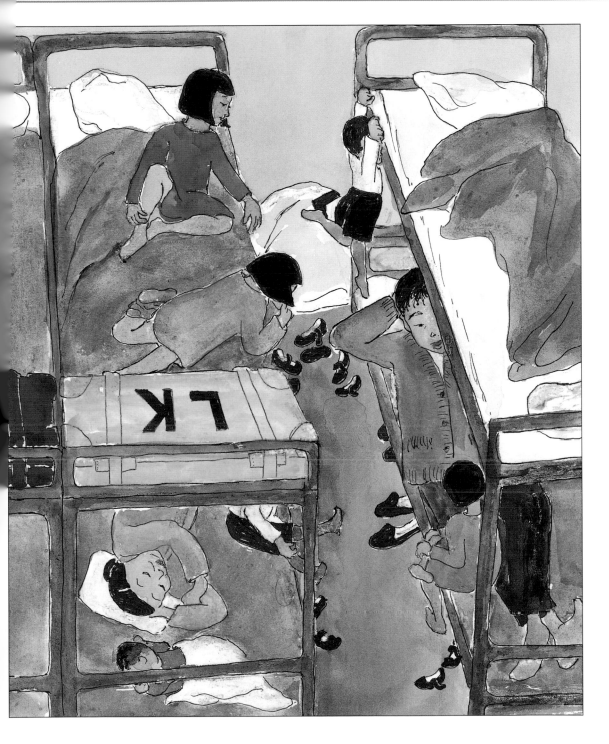

We approached land by night. Next morning, Hong Kong fanned out before us, strange and wonderful. The harbor teemed with all manner of watercraft and was filled with a hubbub of sounds. The city of Victoria, gleaming white in the morning sun, the green peak rising in the background, spirited away memories of the home we had left far behind.

When we disembarked, there was more noise. Hong Kong means 'fragrant port,' but the only nice thing I smelled was the chicken noodle soup at the food stall. All around were the odors of dirty streets, crowds of people, beggars, and sweating coolies straining to pull incredible loads. Through this confusion, Papa attended to our luggage and herded us into a waterfront hotel.

One day, we took a double-decker bus and a cable car up steep Victoria Peak to visit the elegant home of Mr. Kwok. The elaborate carved furniture, the vases, and the figurines all made us feel strange. At first, we were too shy to accept the special food brought by the maid. Oriental luxury was foreign to us.

In fact, all of Hong Kong was foreign, every turn revealing some new wonder. Papa bought cookies and cocoa as surprise treats for Grandmother.

Soon Papa arranged for the short trip to the ferry terminal, where we would continue our journey. Rickshaws were lined up at the curb. Some of the rickshaw boys were sprawled, napping, in their cabs, feet sticking out at the sides. Papa did not disturb them. He engaged three and assigned one to Mama, Lily, and baby Etta; one to me and Gerry; the third to himself with George and Peter.

We climbed onto the wriggly cabs in great anticipation. Papa gave directions. The rickshaw boys grunted answers, got into position, and began their rhythmic jog.

Evening was approaching. Beautiful red bands streaked across the western sky. In the dusky light and the confusion of heavy traffic, all the rickshaws looked alike. Their dark shapes wove in and out, forever moving on and on. *Which one was Papa's?* I lost track, twisting about to peer anxiously into the growing darkness. For the first time since we'd left home, I began to feel panic. If we got separated, I'd still have Gerry, but I wanted Papa. In this strange country, I only felt safe if Papa was with us.

But when we arrived at the terminal, there he was – smiling and coming to help us down.

At last the two-tiered green ferry came in, sliding low on the water. Coolies shouted as they waited with ropes, ready to tie her up. Passengers streamed off, then we boarded. We were shown to a room on the lower deck, covered only with a rattan mat and sprinkled with black block pillows. This was a typical peasant bed, designed for the tropical Kwangtung summers, guaranteed to keep backs straight. We would sleep here for the overnight ride to Canton.

Papa had bought delicious dumplings from a food stall, oozing with sweet black-bean paste, and we ate hungrily.

We neither undressed nor washed. We just took off our shoes and lay down whenever and wherever we felt like it. Through the large open windows, I saw that the face of the man in the moon was getting fat and round, just like it had been when we left home. *Could it be the same one?* I stared up at him, my eyelids heavy, until the lapping of the water and the gentle rocking of the ferry lulled me to sleep.

The Pearl River winds its way into the coastal region of mainland China. The ferry had taken us a distance inland, but we were still far from Grandmother's house.

At the railroad station early next morning, we settled down among the luggage to wait for a train, yawning, unwashed, hungry. A noisy old steam engine finally puffed in, pulling passenger coaches. We climbed aboard. All around us people jostled, laden with string bags, bundles knotted in cloth or tied with ropes, dried salt fish in twine, and coops of clucking chickens. Such loud voices and such odd smells!

We stared as people tossed orange peels and wrapping paper out the window. They stared back at us, foreigners from the Land of the Golden Mountain, pointing to our strange clothes and haircuts.

The home I had known had vanished like smoke, and I was a stranger.

Through the windows we saw rice fields, water buffalo, and farms teeming with ducks. In spite of the rough ride and hard seats, we all began to doze, leaning against each other or on Mama's lap. Late in the afternoon we arrived at Dun Ngan Lai Station. We were oh so tired! The long journey, taking one full cycle of the moon, was nearly over.

On the station platform, Papa stood still in the crisp country air. He must have long dreamed of this return home with his sons to the one place on Earth where he felt he truly belonged. This was where his ancestors, for a thousand years, had had their beginnings and their endings. He looked around him, remembering his boyhood. I had never seen that expression on his face before. *Do grown men cry?* Papa looked close to tears, but soon he smiled. "Let's go to Grandmother's house," he said.

Now began the final walk. Papa led the way between the rice fields, holding his sons by the hand. Mama walked behind him with the baby, while Lily clutched her skirt. Gerry and I trailed them, followed by the coolies. On to the gate of the village. Papa's village. His people. Mother. Forever. Home.

We rounded a corner, turned into a lane, and stepped over Grandmother's high threshold.

There she sat in the courtyard, a grand old lady. She had been waiting all afternoon, wearing her best clothes. Her feet were bound in her best cloths. Her brown face wrinkled up into the loveliest smile I had ever seen.

Suddenly she bent forward and, with one sweeping motion of her long arms, squished all of us to her in a tangle of arms, legs, and bodies. "My heart and liver, my heart and liver, everyone!" she said. "But I'll never remember your names, so I'll just call you my little puppies."

And so she did for the two years we would stay in the village. I snuggled close and thought about the stick figure on the wall in that other world. This was the real thing. This was my grandmother, and I loved her at once.

When night fell, that first night at Grandmother's house, the velvet darkness wrapped itself around us. We lit some small oil lamps and wondered who would sleep where. Papa had said that the man in the moon would travel with us all the way here, and I wondered where he was. I looked up and saw his light through the high window.

Though we were in another world and time, the full moon shone above.